Solace

Mary-Ann Storm

Published by Mary-Ann Storm, 2023.

While every precaution has been taken in the preparation of this book, the publisher assumes no responsibility for errors or omissions, or for damages resulting from the use of the information contained herein.

SOLACE

First edition. July 27, 2023.

ISBN: 979-8223966067

Written by Mary-Ann Storm.

Table of Contents

Solace

The night kisses my face
As I dance underneath a starry sky
I look at its shadows.
With so many questions
Starting with why
My feet feel heavy
Whilst the music plays
I look at the mirrored image.
So sad and miserable
Staring back
As the music keeps playing
Everything inside me
Wish you were here.
It took me back
To all the memories
Of you...
That I hold dear
They're telling me
Do not fear
In it I found solace.
Still with everything in me
I wish you were near
The memories
keeps on raging

They remain vivid and clear.
As I count each falling tear...

Release

Haven't spent time with you, I know
I was too busy taking stock
Of all the turmoil and tears
Plastered in so many ways
Couldn't bring myself to look
You in the eyes
And share these
Maybe I will
Once everything inside me found peace
Just maybe there'll be acceptance of everything.
If I could only regain the energy
For me to release myself...

Into The Wild

Into the wild
As I caress the carcass
Of a Rhino
Blood smeared empty eyes
Now open in the land of the dead
And another tear of hopelessness
Come night
I know I will shed
Into the wild
As the hyaenas laugh echos through
A vacant land
Remnants of slaughter
Still clinging to the blood-stained sand
Into the wild
I go...
Rifle against the shoulder as I walk
I hid beneath the branches.
As if I'm about to stalk
Into the wild, I go
As the lights lit up
another poacher
becomes the prey
In my heart, I'm willing for more poachers to stray

SOLACE

Into the wild
I go...
It's the dance of the ranger
I've come to love and know
Rifle lifted
It's a dance I know
Cause I've learned
As you become one with the night
You have to do it slowly.

My Pink Lady

The trees give a welcoming shade.
As the sun basks on lifted heads
The hands grasping a pink lady
That has ripened over time.
The smell of it
The nicest one can find
Through the laughter and jokes
It is friendships that are bound
All have a pink lady feast in mind
As one they move the bin
A tractor passes and leaves its mark
In the sand
The pink ladies are moved from hand to hand
None of them can end up in the sand.
Everyone knows pink ladies rule the land
They work from morning till noon.
They know the pink ladies
Will give you a reason to smile
And it will have you craving
But not too soon.
In the sun they glistened and gleamed.
While someone is blowing off some steam
Yet the eyes are shining with a proud sheen.
Pink ladies do have such an effect, it seems.

SOLACE

It's the harvest
And the pink ladies
Are glued to its seam
One bite will take you into a sensuous dream

I Gave You

I gave you all I had
My love and warmth
You soaked it up
Drinking from a bottomless cup
I gave you all I had
My attention and energy
You wanted it all.
But in the end, all I gave you
Just wasn't enough
I gave you all I had
My dreams and hopes
You soaked it up
I thought you loved every detail.
That was the story of you and I
Until your expression
Your coldness
Showed me
Everything we shared was a lie.
I gave you all I had
All of me
Without holding back
So losing you
was the one thing
That I didn't expect

SOLACE

I had to pay
To make up for everything you lack
I gave you all I had
Now I'm staring into the depths
Of Darkness
Wishing I could feel less sad...
But I didn't even have the strength.
To be mad...

For You

For you
I'll hold it in
As the shadows cascade in sin
Questions lingering...
Where does righteousness begin?
For you
I'll hold the moon
Leave everything there.
Anger leads to nowhere
Just do self-care
For you ...

Ivory Towers

I dreamt of you
beneath ivory towers
clasp it in my hands
I was drenched in the showers.
My cheeks were wet till the wee hours.
I dreamt of you
beneath ivory towers...
Misty eyes now see clearer
As reality sets in
There's no more room
for what could've been
I know now...
I never should've let you in.

War

There's an ugly side to war.
As the mother weeps
It has no age restriction
Nor the color of one's skin
Not even religions are spared.
It's a battle
Where no one wins
There's an ugly side to war.
As centuries have shown
Where ego's duel
and the hunger for power
A never-ending fuel
Where on both sides
The innocent are mostly slain
Each defender
Becomes the carriers of the same pain
There's an ugly side to war.
Where inhumane acts
It will shake you to the core.
Where the soldier will be a hero
And yet, after centuries,
Could become an outcast
Be labeled a criminal
Just to keep the impact

SOLACE

Of the blame
To a minimal
There's an ugly side to war.
If one can't find common ground
Where gunfire and destruction
Will be a mourner sound
As they visit each grave
Nothing can ever be so profound.
There's an ugly side to war...

My Countryman

In the land of my fathers
I've seen bloodshed.
The unrighteousness co-led
Whilst the wronged cries out to be heard
In the land of my fathers
I've seen so many things.
Through misty eyes
The hope remains
In the end
There'll be happiness in each corner
My countryman brings

Detached

I know you
As doubt creeps in
Just to lay every failure bare
Yet you just sit there.
With an indifferent attitude and stare
Your eyes telling me
You've long since reached a point.
Where you just don't care
I know you
As I search for warmth
That used to engulf the people.
You love
Instead, these days they've encountered
A fist in no need of a glove
I know you
As your eyes coldly survey
Your heart is aligned in a rhythmic sync.
And there's blood dripping on the page.
In the form of ink
I knew you
As the coldness
Shones through
In a stare
A part of you

MARY-ANN STORM

That's urging you on
To bring it all down if you dare
Yet you wonder if ...
If you touch the surface, would it be a big enough scare?
If you dare

Home

I've traced the many steps
The consecutive laps
Somehow, all conjectured into mishaps
Yet my mind wonders
It opens up all the flounders.
They're making me recall all the thunders
As your feet no longer roam in these vacant streets
The recollection of memories filled with laughter
They cause your face to linger long after
My heart bleeds...
Yet at that same instant
I've discovered in those memories
In each corner of my heart
Without you here
I've found a home.

Harvest

Eyes are staring at a wall
In its depths lies no recognition or recall.
The limbs are no longer working
In their perfect form
It's handled with aggressiveness and scorn.
The hands are working quickly
As they move
It's getting rid of any incriminating proof
The movements were secluded and aloof
There'll be no sound chiming from the roof
Quickly, the body is thrown
To the side
Another nameless face to be tagged and hidden
It doesn't matter if the body was mutilated and hagged
Or that it was someone's family or child
It's the harvest
Where only Money Talks
Or the seller walks
Come morning...
The carved
Will latch on to its newest prey
Another harvest
To many just another day...

Covid

I'm Here
Spreading my arms
underneath the rays of the sun
spared through the grace of God
I'm Here
As memories of their eyes, fear-filled
float through my thoughts
and the feeling of hopelessness
filled every being
The question plaguing
Will this be the journey of all?
Our destiny...
I'm Here
As graveyards are overflown
Families snatched away
Who so many wished could stay
I lift my eyes
Heavenwards and I pray
For the ones, I can't help
As well as my own
Once again, it's God's mercy.
That is shown
I'm Here
As I stand

In the aftermath of the turmoil
My being filled
with gratitude and awe
For a Father who still carries me
Whether my world is filled
With darkness or light
There's no need for me to flee.
Or be frightened by the things that I witness or see
I know that under my father's hand, I'm protected.
Through His guidance and love
I'm here...

Life

There's life on the other side of pain
I know...
The sun's rays beneath the clouds
A promise of beauty
Love, laughter, and hope
A vibrant reminder that something beautiful
Will always emerge
No matter what we might face
There's life on the other side of chaos.
I know .....
As nature blooms after the burns
The beauty of a little seed
Canvassing fields for the hungry eye
And a weary heart who needs it
Lifting the spirit
Strengthening and restoring
There's life on the other side of fear
I know...
As I look into the eyes of one
Who has conquered
Had overcome
The eyes always looking heavenwards
Secure in the embrace of a heavenly Father
Who is always in control

MARY-ANN STORM

There's life in the cycles of seasons
I know...
I see it
In the lessons life has taught us
But most of all
Shaped us into who we become
Conquerors, warriors, heroes, and survivors
There's life on the other side of everything.
I know.....
And that's the beauty of life.
because we're all in it
To complete the picture

Hello Beautiful

Hello beautiful
I saw how you rocked that stride.
Your scars open and wide
The blisters are proof you have nothing to hide.
Hello beautiful
I saw how you wiped that floor.
Your body shakes to the rhythm of the beat
Your fierceness and strength
Not allowing you to become a passenger
In the back seat
Hello beautiful
I saw the pain giving way
Whilst determination set in
It was the warrior in you smelling blood
The survivor win
Hello beautiful
I saw how you looked in the mirror.
So collective and calm
Though so many were only there to harm
Your smile for them is a weakness
Under the illusion
You're so easy to fool and charm.
Hello beautiful
I saw how you lifted that sword.

MARY-ANN STORM

Whilst bowing down before God
Paying homage
To the warriors that fell
so obediently waiting to be called
Every attack against you
Will be silenced and slaughtered
With your sword
And everything that was thrown at you
Will fall on the heads of fools
Who mistakenly thought
You were dancing out of your own accord
Hello beautiful
I saw how you rocked that stride.
Your scars open and wide
The blisters are proof you have nothing to hide...

Desert Hinterlands

There are moments of despair.
In the desert hinterlands of my soul
Those moments when I choose
To look
Or dwell there.....
It longs for the people
I loved
The ones I've lost
Yet time passes on.
Like river streams
They're moving forward
Whilst rudely awakening me
From those illicit dreams.....
whilst those stilted memories scream.

Hope

Hope is struggling
through another day
with faith anchored in your soul
scorching my fears into smithereens
Set alight by each undiminishable coal
Hope in the palm
Of your hands
As you gather the strength
to keep believing in your innate purposes
to love, heal, forgive, and embrace
anything that comes your way
Knowing that it'll pass too
Hope is looking at you
and knowing hope is you
Each day, it rises like the morning dew

Just Love

If the world was filled
With just love
Would I have been
Smouldered and shaped
Into the fierce woman
That I am today.
Would my tears
Have been able to dry up
As quickly as it did
As soon as I hear the word maybe...
Would I've been able
To let go
The moment that I needed to
And not dream of an image
Of a white picket fence
and once again with a forlorn heart
Cling to the words of maybe...
Would I've known that the woman
I've become
She is comfortable in her skin.
Understanding that being alone
That doesn't mean that you're not worthy
Instead, it shows maturity.
In the ability that in the silence

MARY-ANN STORM

There are so many things
But most of all, self-worth
That was shaped into something perfect.
Still, if the world was just filled with love
Would I have known?
Just to be can be enough

Lipstick Oasis

I love the way
The softness of your layers
Starts to blossom
Underneath each stroke
As I paint you red
Whilst working upwards
Out of your own accord
Just to add a sparkle to my eyes
Causing it to resonate as if it's adorning
The milky way in the night
Lighting my path just as bright
I love the way
Your fullness grasps the attention
As the colour of pink adorns you
I get at ease.
Spreading love and warmth
With each step
As my hand grasp
Yet another colour
You crave
It's purple I choose
To give you
That feeling of authoritarian
Yet at the same time

To be bold and brave
Now I reach for brown
For today you'd like
To play it safe
I love the way
The softness of your layers
Start to blossom
Sometimes mysterious, sensual
At times quite daring
Yet it's quite normal.
For you to have a lipstick crave
With a radiant smile
I looked in the mirror.
Every outline of my lips
Perfectly coloured
Lines not smeared or out of place
Staring back is a serene and happy face.

Beauty Of Nature

The morning breeze caresses my skin.
I smile at the scent of grass.
Enters my nostrils
Oh the pleasure of early morning
Fresh air thrills
Birds chirping in the trees
The sweetest melodies as they
Fall softly on my accustomed ears
I lift my face towards the sun's rays.
It's wrapping my body in its warmth
Like a giddy child, I'm feeling so comforted
It diminishes all my fears
Tears of happiness are rolling down my face.
It's with gratitude that I lift my arms.
Cause it's the beauty of nature.
I embrace
As I look at the mountains
And trees a river silently passes by
I'm humbled by the beauty it portrays.
Whilst loving the abundance of open space
Nature and I becoming one
Looking at a creation
Such as this
All there's left to feel is safe.

Reverie

To love
Unconditionally
Unashamedly
Painfully
Remorsefully ....
Nonetheless, to love

Beautiful Flowers

Peaceful moments fill the day
beautiful flowers in a full array
Colouring the world
A different beauty
appreciated by all who sees
Whilst feeding the soul
Nature in its purest form
Such a beautiful display
Butterflies flying around
drawn to the nectar
and the sweetness
That it brings
Sunkissed their beautiful wings
Beautiful flowers
Filling the heart
With such calm and joy
The beauty of nature
A reminder
Amidst the chaos
Something beautiful
Can also make its start

South Africa

I remember
How you used to carry yourself
With so much pride
Now you're filled with a callousness
You don't even attempt to hide.
It's ignorance you choose to stride
I remember
There was a time
I mentioned your name.
Boasted with it for all to see
We were one, a message
Throughout the world
It resonated so clearly.
Now when I look at you
I wipe a tear
A rainbow nation just following
It's no longer the cry
For freedom of all that I hear
And as night crawls in
Is it still you that I can hold dear?
When so many are forced
Into uncertainty
Continuously spooned with fear
I remember

SOLACE

A time of freedom and democracy
When all believed the land of milk and honey was so near
Did we lose them all?
Our heroes
Who'd take a stance?
Not once wavering in intimidation
Or be swayed by a stealth glance
I remember...
The graves that made freedom possible for me
And I wonder if this is
What they envisioned our future would one day be.

Masquerade

It's a masquerade
and we all dance
to a melancholic melody
driven by fear as it parks
We're all walking around
With heavy hearts
In the streets reminiscing
If life will offer
A second chance
Throwing at each other
A weary glance
It's a masquerade
Along those silent corridors
all alone
Some eyes are filled with remorse.
Life just wasn't meant to steer so off course.
It's a masquerade
and we all participate
Where the righteous and unrighteous
do battle at an alarming rate
It is the innocent that will suffer.
All castrated in its wake
Or will we stand
So it's not our right.

SOLACE

They so arrogantly take
driven by their own goals
It's the laws they now intend to make.
In which some do not willingly take
It's a masquerade
As the world
Splits into two
I closed my eyes.
And shut it all out
In the silence
I rest assured
That all will be right
Because I'm secured in your power
and might
There's no reason for me to become distressed
Or even do battle
Because you remain the commander of my fight
Always shining bright my Redeemer and light

Two Little Birds

Two little birds came flying my way.
Every morning as the sun rises
They'd chirp their bird song
And come to play
Two little birds
Oh, they seem so frail.
As they fly
From one flower to the other
In the air sticking out a tail
Two little birds
drawn to the nectar
That each flower brings
And as I watched them
All I hear is the way they sing.
Once again, I'm humbled
By their appearance
As each spread a wing
Two little birds
What a beautiful sight
So in tune with nature
They add something special
To another day
As they fly around chirping
The sun starts to shine extra bright

SOLACE

Everything that weighed me down
On the inside, it dissipates
And, once again, my soul is filled with light.

If Words Tend To Fail

If words tend to fail
and you can't seem to find
Anything worth saying
you've known pain
Walking underneath the spray of the rain
and all you could claim
Was the cold rejection inside yourself
In repetition, discovering you're whispering your name
If words tend to fail
And you can't find
Anything worth saying
you've known pain
Walking underneath the spray of the rain
and you've discovered
There's no prison worse than self-blame.
If words tend to fail
and you can't seem to find
Anything worth saying
you've known pain
Walking underneath the spray of the rain
But so will the sun as morning comes.
and you'll realize that you are imperfect
Doesn't put you to shame.
There's nothing wrong with becoming undone

Jumping Castle

Jumping Castle
Here I come
Hippity hop
Hippity top
Jumping Castle
Jumping Castle
Jumping Castle
Here I come
Hippity hop
Hippity top

Jumping Castle
Here I am
Hippity hop
Hippity top
Orange, Yellow, Green, Purple
Bouncing on the walls
Hippity hop
Hippity top
Twirling, screaming, jumping on
Red, Pink, Blue, Grey
Hippity hop
Hippity top

Jumping Castle
Jumping high
Jumping low
Springing, bouncing, sailing down
Shoes flying out
Flip flop
Hippity hop
Hippity top

Jumping Castle
Jumping high
Jumping low
Singing, laughing, hands in the air
Diving down soft bumps
Hippity hop
Hippity top

Jumping Castle
Jumping high
Jumping low
Falling against colored walls
Pulling playing in the crowd
Jumping is just so much fun.
Hippity hop
Hippity top

Jumping Castle
Jumping high
Jumping low

SOLACE

Feeling a little tired now
From jumping up and down
Hippity hop
Hippity top

Jumping Castle
Jumping high
Jumping low
See you next time
When the sun shines
have to find my flip-flops
Hippity hop
Hippity top

Here I am
Hippity hop
Hippity top
Orange, Yellow, Green, Purple
Bouncing on the walls
Hippity hop
Hippity top
Twirling, screaming, jumping on
Red, Pink, Blue, Grey
Hippity hop
Hippity top
Jumping Castle
Jumping high
Jumping low
Springing, bouncing, sailing down
Shoes flying out

MARY-ANN STORM

Flip flop
Hippity hop
Hippity top
Jumping Castle
Jumping high
Jumping low
Singing, laughing, hands in the air
Diving down soft bumps
Hippity hop
Hippity top
Jumping Castle
Jumping high
Jumping low
Falling against colored walls
Pulling playing in the crowd
Jumping is just so much fun.
Hippity hop
Hippity top
Jumping Castle
Jumping high
Jumping low
Feeling a little tired now
From jumping up and down
Hippity hop
Hippity top
Jumping Castle
Jumping high
Jumping low
See you next time
When the sun shines

SOLACE

have to find my flip-flops
Hippity hop
Hippity top

I've Bled You Know

I've bled, you know.
A thousand times
In those silent moments
Screaming back at me
And I'd whisper
Just let me be
I've bled, you know.
As morning came
Stilling those memories
Enflinched in my mind
I often look at them.
As they rewind
And I whisper
Give me rest
Is it in you to spare me some?
I've bled, you know.
As the evening came
Looking at the entrance
As the day is done
Thought I saw you there
But you vanished without a care
I've bled, you know.
A thousand times
And I know some things may never be done

SOLACE

With saddened eyes
I greet the sun behind the mountains
As it rises
Another morning without you has come

Just A Little Note

Just a little note
to help you cope
and a reminder
that there's always hope
so that you may always
Find in stormy waters
a rescuing rope
enabling you to start from a clean slope.

Curious World

Curious eyes looking at the road
Little hands waving and swinging through the air
Excitedly at the road, they stare
On he moves without care.
It's time to visit the station
Now there must be something there.
It's choo-choo sounds
And a railway, it seems.
The discovery of a train and its steam
What could be missing?
The little one wonders while sitting
Could it be colored blocks?
Where you can build all sorts
Of stuff while you explore
Now happily creating whatever comes to mind
All done now, it's taken apart.
It's more fun.
Laughing little feet now running
Time for another adventure to start
Now what can be more fun?
Then the motorbike ride
It's laughter and contentment
Underneath blue skies
It's green grass and riding

MARY-ANN STORM

In the shades of the trees
Still, another adventure awaits.
Now what should be explored next?
It's the curious world of a child
What did you expect?

Tears From Heaven

Forever and a day
Lying awake listening to the falling rain
Forever and a day
It's a welcoming blessing I'd say,
Forever and a day
Looking towards a clouded sky
Forever and a day
It's tears from heaven
Our land no longer appears dry.
Forever and a day
The mountain tops are beautiful and wet
Forever and a day
We're humbled and no longer driven by respect.
Now we know to turn to God instead.
Forever and a day
Lying awake listening to the falling rain
Forever and a day
It's a welcoming blessing I'd say,
Everything is possible once you start to pray

Silence

Silence....
Who knew it could make a sound?
Deafening in its aftermath
In its embrace, solitary is what I found.
Silence....
Who knew it could speak?
The sound of messages is now louder than before.
In unguarded moments, shaking you to the core
Silence....
Who knew it could be a signal too?
Footsteps sound dimmer until they fade away.
Until you realize there was nothing
That you could do
It wasn't in your power to make him stay.
Silence ....
Who knew it could be a history book?
Memories flooding tearing you apart
Still for me, out of the numbness
My life has to start
Didn't matter how long it would take
Silence....
Who knew it could say so much?
It's the miss you moments
That never seems to fade.

SOLACE

For a departure
There was never a decision left for anyone to make.

In Loving Memory of My Father Jan Baron

Giants

Do we listen to them, those Giants?
The ones who silently fought
and dared to voice concerns
For the ones walking around distraught
Do we listen to them, those Giants?
The ones who loudly declare
Unfairness in the open air
Or do we ignore the voiceless
When it's not their sentiments we share
Do we listen to them?
The ones who crossed the Borders
So we could be heard
So no one is forced to wear an invisible shirt.
Do we listen to them, those Giants?
The ones who silently fought
For our rights to speak
Who gave courage to the weak?
Or, in the end, is it righteousness?
We all still seek

Commune

My community never sleeps
Day and night time
They know of the stranger who weeps
My community never sleeps
Guarding and never missing a thing
They have a thousand tales to tell.
If you wish well
It harbors so many secrets.
That it keeps
My community never sleeps
They know of every stranger and scar
Every license plate or car
And of the one who in the street bleeds
My community never sleep
They stand guard day and night.
There are so many underlying battles.
They have to fight
Still, it's their own they'll protect and keep.

Heels

She wore them daily.
Without complaint
I'd thought it'd break
Her different heels
Now I've discovered it's encased with steel
See-through fog through rain
She'll never express what she feels
Still, she wore proudly those heels.
Instilled from birth is a woman
Made out of steel
See we ladies seldom express
Just how we feel
It doesn't matter how many layers
You'd think
You'd peel
She'll be wearing those painted heels.
You'll always be guessing.
As to what it is she feels
And see it's never disrespect
It's an innate strong centered will
And you'll realize
The lady is in control still

Who's To Blame

Who's to blame?
As the world weeps
And each wound cuts deep
When all live in fear
As if all would become slaughtered sheep
Who's to blame?
As the world weeps
And each wound cuts deep
And none sleep
Yet in the heart
Uncertainty flourishes and creeps
Is it our Saviour that we seek?
When the language of pain is all of which
We continuously speak
Who's to blame?
As the world weeps
And each wound cuts deep....

The Journey

In the smallest gesture lies the memories
Written on the contours of the heart
Through time embedded in the soul
A point from which we all start
Without it, nothing could be regarded as a whole.
Still in unguarded moments
Like a kiss through the lens
Are those beautiful moments we stole?

Echo's

An empty house with no picture frames
The echo vibrates off the clean walls
Feet remain invisible yet still carry
Through the open doors
Still, through echoes, the memory stalls.
Each room has a story to tell.
It's all about arrival and departure entwined
The nourishing tales of laughter, pain
And wishing you well
Echo's still calling through the fog and rain
Some echoes only recall pain
Attached to an unknown name
Still, the echo resounds just the same

Into The Blue

Into the Blue
Arms spiraling out
Threading on the ocean waves
While the tides carry me
The eruption of laughter is so giddish and free.
Happiness evoked by the passers who see
Into the Blue
It's the artist and dreamer that reaches
Always provoking a scholar and free minds
Still, it's the dreamer who teaches.

Amazed

Little feet running around
Uplifting moments
Lightening the heart
Curious eyes searching around
The laughter of a child
Keeping me home ground
Little feet running around
While surrounded by bridges and sand
Ploughing and building
With joyful sounds
Warmth is all you'll find.
In a children's land
Little feet running around
Chasing a cat
Across wooden floors and grass
Children's laughter enlightens the ones who pass
Little feet running around
A joy to the heart
With their beautiful souls
A reminder of innocence
A point from which we all start

First Love

Did you ever crave that feeling of bewilderment?
So amazed at how strong and deep it went.
Were your cheeks ever wetted by tear stains?
Did you ever feel cleansed?
Through heaven rains
Did you ever bow with the faith of a child?
And felt a caress so ever mild
It's an old familiar feeling
Of a first love anchored
Forevermore in the faith of a child
No longer bleeding

Daybreak

Daybreak found me looking at the mountaintops
Pen and paper clutched like a forlorn friend
I watched as the colors painted the sky.
And once again, I'm plagued by questions.
And so many whys
And I miss you past these silent tears.
It's a feeling I've become accustomed to over the years.
You're no longer there to placate my fears.
I miss you as my unsteady hand refuses to write
The wrinkled tear-stained paper
No longer appear unused and so white
I wonder if I could ever capture
Any reasoning or plight
My eyes once again search for courage
To pin a letter down
As weary eyes drift in the direction of the town
Once again, I'm waiting for that.
The familiar beep of a message to come
In the silence I accepted
I knew there would be none.
I miss you as my week starts.
When it ends
There'll be no more.
I love you, Anne

MARY-ANN STORM

Or how have you been?
The messages you can no longer send
And I hope it's a pain that time will mend.
Am I happy that you know the truth?
Sometimes I wonder if it was worth the pain.
As I walk drenched in the rain
I miss you, Dad
Wish you could tell me, then I'd stop feeling so sad.

Angel Eyes

When you wave goodbye
Don't weep for me
The child asked me to let it be
Angel eyes wisely scolding me
Still, when I look at innocence, it is all I see.
When you wave goodbye
Don't weep for me
The little hands remain strong.
In the smile a message so clear
An Angel accepted heaven was where she belonged
Still, when I look at innocence, it is all I see.
The child doesn't share my fear
When you wave goodbye
Don't weep for me
Angel eyes asking to be set free
The child let me know it wasn't about me.
Still, when I look at innocence, it is all I see.
When you wave goodbye
Don't weep for me
I'm at peace, can't you see?
Angel, eyes till the end, remains alive
Still, when I look at innocence, it is all I see.
Towards us for hope, peace, and love
We all strive

MARY-ANN STORM

In heaven, a child is set free
For all children fighting cancer

66

Pure Inspiration

For the love of writing
I scribble on you
The lines are more apparent
How could I have left you for so long?
Through our never-ending conversations
I grew strong
In haste, I will pin a note to you.
Blue lines and white embracing each other
Still, you never flinch over my tirades.
My perfect companion
With you, I can laugh, cry, and be angry.
You never mind
It's the artist's soul combined with yours.
How do you tolerate me?
It's a mystery in itself.
But you accept me even while I delve
You never let me be
Words dancing through forests
Revealing the mystery of distant worlds
Where everything can be magically arranged
It's a place where not one story
Ever appear strange
With arms lifted high
I began to smile.

MARY-ANN STORM

While the sunlight enlightens me
The artist is now completely free.
We always find something beautiful.
Or maybe it's just me.
You soak it all up.
The laughter, wisdom, and pain
A forever true companion
There's no time for feeling blue
This morning I woke up and realized
There are no more clouds
While I wasn't looking, it stopped raining.

Star Struck

Gosh! couldn't be
Fluttering eyelashes
That's me?
Wait!
Come closer
this, I need to see
Gosh! couldn't be
Wearing mini skirts and high heels
Miss Exotic that's me?
Wait!
Come closer
this, I need to see
Oh my!
I guess that's how fame must feel.
Gosh! couldn't be
Miss Sexy who just snaps her fingers
and she has it?
Wait!
Come closer
to this, I need to see
You're telling me about this dazzling creature.
seems to be roaming free?
Gosh! couldn't be
She's turning heads.

just walking the line?
Wait!
Come closer
this, I need to see
Someone is under the impression
She's mighty fine.
Oh my!
I knew that stranger wasn't me.
Gosh! couldn't be
How am I supposed to compete with that?
She sounds captivating
Full of mischief and adventure
Wait!
Come closer
to this, I need to see
It's a sin for such a creature to be roaming free.
But I still chose good old me
Gosh! couldn't be
You're telling me she is me?
Yet still roaming free?
Once she's finished signing autographs
This is one woman I need to meet and see.
Tell me if she is me.
Yet still roaming free?
Once she

Street Corners

Questioning eyes looking at me
Frail shoulders demanding an answer
Insisting what do you see?
The clothing has seen better days.
In the cold, searching for a warm place
The eyes now hardened in the child's face.
Saying keep your distance
I want no pity to embrace
The bare feet washed by the rain
The proudness still strong and hidden is the pain
Yet he's still demanding what do you see?
Now they're screaming you don't know me
If you're coming with your cameras and charity cases
Me on the front plastered
While they call it shame....shame.
They won't even remember my name.
The angered eyes told me I didn't want instant fame.
Just take your gifts if this is your game.
Frail shoulders now standing tall
Eyes still questioning what do you see?
I answered a person in need
I don't need you to bleed
Taking the package, he finally smiled.
He sustained injuries that weren't mild.

Driving away in the rear mirror
He showed me the child.

Tapper

Little feet tapper
still
tipper
tapper
tip
a
tap
Hush now little one
time to take a nap
Little feet tapper
still
Giddy eyes
sparkling still
tipper
tapper
tap
Full laughter fills every room
Little eyes now more awake
No longer taking a nap
Tipper
tapper
tip
a tap
A world of adventure awaits

MARY-ANN STORM

Baby eyes exploring the rooms
with childish enthusiasm
in little hands
the so loved map
Little feet
tapper still
tipper
tapper
tip
a tap
running, screaming, laughing,
and toys lying around in disarray
warmth filling the room
Little feet tapper
still
no one will be sleeping soon

Flight

Beneath blue skies
You take your route
In haste, you reach out
To help the helpless hand
One of our selfless souls
That still roams our land.
Beneath blue skies
You take your flight
A beacon of hope
For the stranded in the night
Our angels walking in the light
Beneath blue skies
A warm heartthrobs
Belying the tired eyes
Alerted and with precision hands, are checking the probs
Beneath blue skies
You swept by
Rushing with your special cargo
There's no time to waste
If only we all hungered
and had a Samaritan heart
Your presence dims all the cruelty and lies.

MARY-ANN STORM

For all the medical staff working over the festive season and responding to daily emergencies

Seasons

Autumn leaves
how familiar you seem
dancing to the tunes of the wind
gracefully you float
for all to be seen
Your rich color is so beautiful and warm.
yet you know
how to handle every windy storm
Quietly, Winter steps in
Another wonder
Its beauty is immaculate.
always remaining for those who have seen
Now there's a spring in my step.
in amazement, soaring on an eagle's wing
Excitement is what you bring.
In summer, it is the melodies
of praise that I sing
cascading and spiraling
in joyful rays
enjoying each season in different ways

Color Blind

Freedom!
Freedom!
I can still hear them shout.
For you and I
They marched in unison.
and remained color blind
To create freedom in my mind
Freedom!
Freedom!
I can still hear them shout.
For you and I
They marched in unison.
and remained color blind
Brothers and sisters with different skin tones
All the unmarked history of graves never mentioned the unnamed
Yet it is their legacy we have claimed
Freedom!
Freedom!
I can still hear them shout.
For you and I
They marched in unison.
and remained color blind
They were forced to recognize

SOLACE

That problem that still clouds our minds
When they cried, their tears were the same.
Never did they cast any blame
Freedom!
Freedom!
I can still hear them shout.
For you and I
They marched in unison.
and remained color blind
All of them carrying some sort of pain.
Their blood didn't ask for skin color or name
When we look back now
Did they make those sacrifices in vain?

Naked

Naked
Faces cast away
Naked
In the aftermath
Naked
Either pay the price or don't stay.
Naked
There are no blurred colored lines.
Naked
They know how to walk around landmines.
Naked
For the world to see
Naked
They still chose just to be
Naked
They're the only ones who can break
the silence
To be free

A Bird

A bird does not fly
The wind is blowing the plant's stem
Whilst the sun is shining

Blue

I'm feeling blue
Blue Blue
Without you to lighten my way
I'm Feeling blue-blue
Without you
Still, there's nothing I...
Can do
all images of you
starts to vaporize
Into a sky so blue
And there's nothing I can do.
My world is painted blue

Don't miss out!

Visit the website below and you can sign up to receive emails whenever Mary-Ann Storm publishes a new book. There's no charge and no obligation.

https://books2read.com/r/B-A-SKLF-LCFMC

BOOKS 2 READ

Connecting independent readers to independent writers.

About the Author

Mary-Ann Storm is a Journalist and writer from South Africa. She was born in Ceres but grew up in the Overberg Region in the Western Cape.